In Quin's Room

By Carmel Reilly

It is wet!

Quin sits on the bed.

Quin's bed

Quin has a pad on his lap.

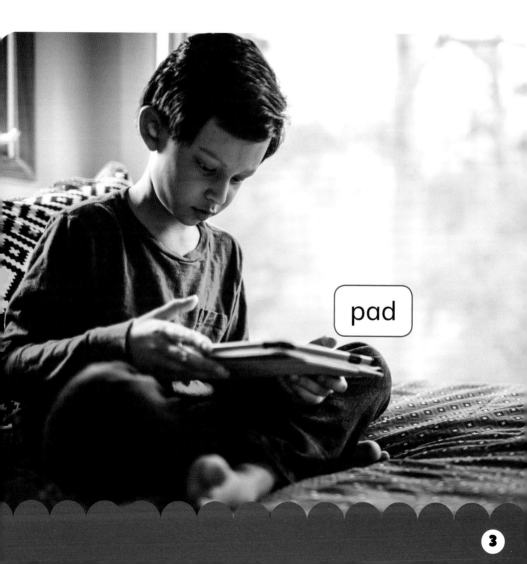

pad

Quin can see his bag on the rug.

bag

rug

He can see his map kit
and a red pen.

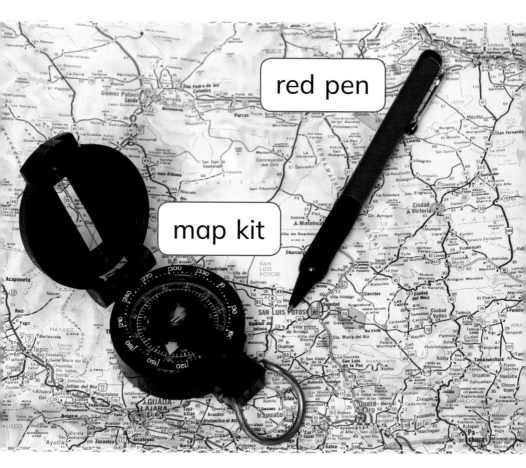

red pen

map kit

Quin can see his jet, van and tug.

jet

van

tug

He can see pads and lots of pens in a tub.

pads

pens

tub

Quin can see Kit Cat!

Kit Cat

It is not wet.

Quin can see the sun.

Kit Cat can see the sun, too!

CHECKING FOR MEANING

1. What sort of kit can Quin see? *(Literal)*

2. Where are Quin's pens? *(Literal)*

3. Do you think Quin likes being inside on a rainy day? Why? *(Inferential)*

EXTENDING VOCABULARY

Quin's	Why is there an apostrophe and an *s* after Quin's name in the title? What does the *s* show belongs to Quin?
has, his	Say the words *has* and *his*. Which sounds are the same in both words? Which sounds are different?
kit, Kit	The word *kit* is used in the book with a capital letter, as in *Kit Cat*, and without a capital letter, as in *map kit*. Explain the different meanings of the word *kit* in the book.

MOVING BEYOND THE TEXT

1. If the book went for another page, what do you think Quin would do next? Why?

2. What do you like to do when it is raining outside?

3. What do you like to do when it is sunny outside?

4. What would you see in your room if you were inside on a rainy day?

SPEED SOUNDS

Kk	Ll	Vv	Qq	Ww
Dd	Jj	Oo	Gg	Uu
Cc	Bb	Rr	Ee	Ff	Hh	Nn
Mm	Ss	Aa	Pp	Ii	Tt

Quin

wet

lap

van

kit

lots

Kit